Rise to Your Money Power

A Step-by-Step Guide
for Building the Foundation of an
Empowered Relationship with Money

Pamela Plick

Crescendo
PUBLISHING

Rise to Your Money Power
By Pamela Plick

Copyright © 2020 by Pamela Plick

Crescendo Publishing, LLC
2-558 Upper Gage Ave., Ste. 246
Hamilton, ON L8V 4J6
Canada

GetPublished@CrescendoPublishing.com
1-877-575-8814

ISBN: 978-1-948719-22-3 (P)
ISBN: 978-1-948719-23-0 (E)

Printed in the United States of America
Cover design by Anointing Productions

10 9 8 7 6 5 4 3 2 1

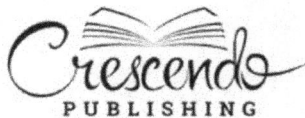
Crescendo PUBLISHING

A Gift from the Author

I believe in you and want to support you in your MONEY POWER journey, so I have prepared some additional resources to help you implement the action steps presented in the book.

Get instant access to the complementary materials here:

http://www.pamelaplickauthor.com/

Table of Contents

Dedication

This book is dedicated to….

My son, Frank, who inspires me every day and is the light of my life.

The phenomenal women in my life—my teachers, mentors, friends, and family—who inspired and encouraged me to amplify my voice.

You, the reader, for choosing to create greater independence and confident movement in your life by your desire to build a more empowered relationship with your money.

WOMEN. MONEY. POWER.

Now is the time for women to stand strong in their relationship with money, because it is the gateway to greater independence and confident, forward movement.

Why I Wrote This Book

I wrote this book because I deeply desire to inspire a cultural shift in the consciousness of women. I hope to help them transform their relationship with money so they can rise to their MONEY POWER by overcoming limiting beliefs, challenges, and self-sabotage related to their work, money, and purpose.

Through the pages of this book, you will learn not only from my personal journey, but also my experience, knowledge, and expertise gained during my more than 30 years in the industry and working with hundreds of women. Because what I know is that when women understand the steps they can take to eliminate worry out of building financial independence, they can better focus on bringing their gifts into the world to have the greatest impact.

By reading this book, I want you to become more self-aware, create greater financial balance, and transform your personal relationship with money by becoming more confident and ready to take inspired action.

I want you to know the shift starts with transforming the beliefs and mindsets that no longer serve you.

You will experience this shift as you gain the knowledge to rise to your own MONEY POWER and complete each of the five steps:

Step 1: Create a new relationship with money
Step 2: Nurture a prosperity mindset
Step 3: Empower yourself through financial education
Step 4: Take inspired action
Step 5: Create a Money Power Manifesto

In order to make positive movement in our personal, professional, and financial journey, we must take action. So, at the end of each step, I have included an "action steps" section to give you some highly valuable action steps you can take at each phase to move yourself forward. This section helps you apply what you learn in each chapter to your own life. It will also be helpful for you to start a MONEY POWER journal and write down your insights as you complete your action steps.

I would like to mention this book is designed to provide financial education and should not be considered financial planning or investment advice.

I also want to mention although this book is written for women, men can gain value from it as well.

Pamela Plick

Introduction

My MONEY POWER Journey

My MONEY POWER journey began over 30 years ago. Despite having a great job, I—like so many other women—found myself in an uncertain and scary place after my divorce. With a young child to care for, I needed to understand how to plan for my family's future; I needed to take control of my money and life.

Although I was a saver, I really didn't know much about building wealth. Early in my career, with the common misconception that I couldn't afford it, I did not initially contribute to my company's 401(k) plan. A caring manager advised me that by not contributing, I was giving away free money. This piece of advice resonated with me and would be the foundation for my approach to financial planning and education. I was so appreciative that my manager took the time to explain how the company plan worked and how I could build wealth over time.

Inspired by his advice, not only did I begin to contribute to the company 401(k) plan, but it ignited and fueled a sincere curiosity in building financial security. I wanted to learn more, and that's exactly what I did. I immersed myself in learning everything I could about financial planning, investing, and building financial security.

After completing my undergraduate degree in business administration with a major in finance and a minor in accounting, I completed the advanced education that led me to become a CERTIFIED FINANCIAL PLANNER (CFP)™ practitioner. Because I wanted to expand my practice to help more women, I also became a Certified Money Coach (CMC)®.

During my journey and as I progressed in my career, I found that too many women carry limiting beliefs around money.

As I progressed in my career, I met numerous women like me who, due to limiting money beliefs, divorce, loss of their spouse, or simply a lack of engagement in their family finances, found themselves lacking confidence in successfully managing their money and securing a plan for their future.

At one time or another, many of us experience a fear or lack of confidence around money that not only keeps us from stepping into our MONEY POWER and achieving our goals, but prevents us from living our dreams and the life we deserve. In addition, for those of us who are or aspire to be entrepreneurs, it blocks us from getting the vital funding we require to flourish in our business. In fact, although women are starting more businesses in the United States than ever before, fewer women receive business financing versus our male counterparts.

Once I established my own firm, I made it my mission to help purpose-driven professional and entrepreneurial women overcome challenges or self-sabotage related to their work, money, and purpose by providing education, strategies, and tools to grow financial confidence, independence, and freedom. For some of my clients, I act as an educator—for others, a coach or mentor. For all of my clients, I am a trusted partner who empowers them to take control of their money.

Welcome to **RISE TO YOUR MONEY POWER** ... *a step-by-step guide for building the foundation of an empowered relationship with money.*

Chapter 1

Stop Giving Away Your Money Power

IN THIS CHAPTER, YOU WILL:

- **Learn** why too many women give away their MONEY POWER.
- **Discover** the key ways we give away MONEY POWER.
- **Define** the significant actions you can immediately take to stop giving away your MONEY POWER.

Far too many women for far too long have given away their power in their relationship with money. But the fact is, we do this without even knowing.

As women, we have historically been the nurturers in the family. We take care of everyone's needs—even to the point of putting others' needs ahead of our own. Culturally, a lot of women have been taught that it is the responsibility of the father or spouse to handle the family's finances. In fact, it wasn't until 1974 that women could even get credit in their own name. Fortunately, times have changed.

Everyone faces challenges in achieving their long-term financial goals, such as a successful retirement. But women seem to have a few unique obstacles to overcome. Fortunately, women can alleviate these challenges through financial planning and implementing a strategy.

I believe the three biggest challenges that women face when it comes to money matters are:

1. Unpredictable life events
2. Economic realities and retirement planning hurdles
3. Giving away MONEY POWER

Unpredictable Life Events

On average, women will be on their own financially for one-third of their adult lives. Approximately 50 percent of marriages end in divorce. And, according to wiserwomen.org, a third of women who become widowed are younger than age 60.

Half of all women who will become widowed become so by age 65. In fact, the average age of widowhood is 59 (according to the U.S. Census).

Economic Realities and Retirement Planning Hurdles

It is so important to consider the economic realities and retirement planning hurdles when planning for a successful retirement. Such as:

- *Longer life expectancies* - On average, we live five years longer than men, which means we need to plan for a longer rather than shorter retirement.

- *Lower earnings* - On average, we earn less than men in the workplace. According to the Women's Institute for a Secure Retirement (WISER), men out-earn women an average of 22 to 23 cents on the dollar. Lower earnings result in less money contributed to retirement plans and social security.

- *More time out of the workforce* - We typically are the caregivers. We may spend time out of the workforce to raise a family or care for ailing parents or other relatives. This time away can potentially negatively impact raises and promotions. In addition, while we are out of the workforce, we are not contributing to our pensions, other retirement plans, or social security—which means we end up with less in savings than our male counterparts.

Giving Away MONEY POWER

Situations sometimes arise in which we create additional barriers between us and our goals by giving away our MONEY POWER.

I'm here to say: **it's time to end this**.

Five key ways women give away their MONEY POWER are:

1. Letting someone else take care of your finances
I have seen this quite often over the years: Women (and some men) who are completely unengaged around their finances. You should not completely turn over the responsibility for managing your finances to anyone—including an advisor, spouse, family member, friend, etc. First of all, by putting someone else in charge of your finances, you are making them solely responsible for your financial future. It's okay to have someone who has the knowledge and expertise to manage your finances, but you need to be a partner in the process. Stay informed and engaged around your money so you can empower yourself with the knowledge to make informed financial decisions.

2. Being too conservative with your investments

On average, we typically live longer than men—so our investments need to last longer. The risk of being overly conservative with your investments is that you could potentially outlive your money. You should invest based on your risk tolerance and time horizon, but not be overly conservative. At least part of your portfolio should be invested for growth. If you don't understand what's in your portfolio, make an appointment with your advisor to have them explain your investments to you. You may not know all of the ins and outs of the investments, but you need to know your investment strategy and why.

3. Supporting your children's needs over your own

We tend to put other people's needs before our own, especially our children. It is only natural that you want to help your children, but what do you do when your adult child wants (or needs) to move back home? Or, what if they constantly need financial assistance from you? When it comes to adult children, the best gift you can give them is to be financially independent and not be a burden to them later in life. It's important not to give away assets that you may need down the road, or that will potentially put your financial security in jeopardy should you relinquish them. One of the ways you can help your adult children is by paying the cost of your child working with a financial professional to create a long-term plan, especially if debt is involved.

4. Not talking to your spouse or significant other about financial matters

I have worked with numerous couples over the years who were not on the same page regarding their finances. In this situation, there is usually one spouse who takes care of the finances in the family, and the other spouse for whatever reason is not engaged.

In addition, we, as women, sometimes have a tendency of not wanting to talk with our significant other about financial matters. It is so important to initiate a conversation because it helps you to:

- *Understand each other's perceptions about money* - We have all heard the saying "opposites attract." This is also true in how couples perceive and manage their money. What happens when you are the saver and your mate likes to spend? It is important to understand each other's perceptions and beliefs about money so you can come to a mutual solution.

- *Make sure you both are on the same page* - It is important that you both understand the family finances and are able to set goals as a couple. You both need to be on the same page regarding spending and budgeting. Even though you both may have different target dates for retirement, you both should agree about how much of the household budget you will be saving toward retirement or other major goals.

- *Be prepared in the event of an emergency* - Even though one of you may be primarily responsible for balancing the checkbook or paying the bills, it is critical that you both take the time to understand where you are financially. You should know where the important documents such as insurance papers, investment statements, etc. are located. Either of you should be able to step in and be knowledgeable about everything, from the monthly budget to insurance and investments.

Be proactive with your significant other when it comes to talking about money. This not only helps you grow together financially, but it also is another way to show your love for your mate.

5. Procrastinating on financial decisions
What is the #1 reason many women are hesitant about making financial decisions?

The fear of making a mistake.

One of the main obstacles to women planning effectively for their long-term financial goals is procrastination. Women sometimes tend to put off making important financial decisions due to a lack of confidence. Typically, the lack of confidence is due to the fear of making a mistake. You can easily overcome this obstacle by educating yourself.

Because approximately 90 percent of women will be on their own financially at least once in their lives, it is critical that women make smart choices when it comes to their finances.

Some significant actions you can take to immediately stop giving away your MONEY POWER include:

- Educate yourself by reading and attending workshops
- Take an active role in your investments, including your retirement plans
- Invest for long-term growth
- Maximize your contributions to your retirement plan
- Review your social security benefits
- Consider working with a financial planner

It is important for you to remember that you are in control of your financial future. Financial education and careful planning can go a long way toward helping you avoid giving away your MONEY POWER, achieve your long-term financial goals, and live the lifestyle you desire (and deserve).

Chapter 2

Rise to Your Money Power

IN THIS CHAPTER, YOU WILL:

- **Gain** access to a step-by-step model for rising to your MONEY POWER.
- **Develop** an understanding of the **Facets of MONEY POWER**, the aspects that comprise your relationship with money.
- **Begin** to build the foundation for creating an empowered relationship with money.

One of the things women need most today is a step-by-step education in ways to define and refine their relationship with money.

Once we begin to rise to our MONEY POWER, we step into our sweet-spot of recognizing, rising, and standing in our power by overcoming our limiting beliefs, challenges, and self-sabotage related to our work, money, and purpose. By doing this, we can find the inspiration and confidence to bring our gifts into the world in ways that have the greatest impact.

Rising to your MONEY POWER is not about how much money you have. In this book, I offer a five-step model for building your MONEY POWER foundation and creating greater confidence and forward movement:

Step 1: Create a New Relationship with Money (Chapter 3)
Step 2: Nurture a Prosperity Mindset (Chapter 4)
Step 3: Empower Yourself through Financial Education and Support (Chapter 5)
Step 4: Take Inspired Action (Chapter 6)
Step 5: Create a MONEY POWER MANIFESTO (Chapter 7)

When we talk about money, we usually focus on the practical side. Honestly, most of us know the importance of knowing where our money goes, saving money for a rainy day, and not becoming overextended.

If we know what we should *be doing financially, why are we not taking the steps to get our finances in order?*

There are three **Facets of MONEY POWER**, the aspects that comprise your relationship with money, that you should develop an understanding of:

- Spiritual
- Emotional
- Practical

If we need healing in any of the aspects, it can prevent us from confidently moving forward and rising in our MONEY POWER.

Spiritual

If you desire to live a spiritual life, you know that means to live an abundant life. Living an internal abundant life gives you the power to create abundance in the form of money and outer wealth. Increased financial resources give you the opportunity to have many life experiences. In addition, money is one tool you can use to do more good in the world.

Emotional

Have you ever purchased anything on the spur of the moment (such as a dress or pair of shoes), then realized you didn't really like or need it when you got home? Everyone wants to make smart financial decisions, but unfortunately, we sometimes allow our emotions to take the lead. There are times in which if you allow your emotions to lead your financial decisions, it can have a negative impact on your financial situation.

Which emotions do you allow to influence your financial decisions?

- Anxiety
- Fear
- Anger
- Grief
- Guilt
- Boredom
- Jealousy
- Feeling overwhelmed
- Feeling too confident

The good news is, by recognizing and understanding these behaviors and emotions, you can control them and avoid making poor financial decisions that could negatively affect your financial future. If you can identify them, stop before you make a decision and think, *Am I making this decision based on sound information, or am I allowing my emotions to get in the way?*

Practical

The practical aspect of your relationship with money consists of taking the necessary steps to move forward. If you know the steps you need to take—such as creating your budget, consistently saving, and reviewing your investment statements—but are not doing them, then you want to look at what is preventing you from moving forward.

To begin to build the foundation for creating a more empowered relationship with money, contemplate what current belief(s) you may have within each of the three aspects that may be preventing you from creating the life you desire.

Chapter 3

STEP ONE:
Create a New Relationship
with Money

IN THIS CHAPTER, YOU WILL:

- **Examine** your current relationship with money and why it is important that you develop an empowered relationship.
- **Gain** clarity and a better understanding about why you make the money decisions you do.

- **Identify** ways you can begin to create a new relationship with money.

I truly believe that our personal relationship with money directly impacts how successful we are in our personal and professional lives.

The first step to rising to your MONEY POWER is to examine your current relationship with money. Do you know why you make the money decisions you do?

Most of our money beliefs can be traced back to our childhood. These beliefs were "imprinted" upon us by our parents (usually) or another authority figure who influenced us as we grew up. In order to understand and change your (limiting) beliefs about money, you need to go within.

"Life is like an onion. You peel it off one layer at a time, and sometimes you weep."
- Carl Sandburg

As you go within, you begin to peel away the layers of your money story. As you peel, it may trigger painful memories. You begin to reveal how these triggers are impacting you today. You get to your core and begin to live an authentic life that reflects who you truly are.

What is your earliest or most significant memory of money?

Although I don't remember my earliest memory of money, I do remember one of my most significant memories as a child. I don't recall my parents ever giving me an allowance, but I did have a piggy bank. I believe I was about nine or ten when my grandmother, Martha, opened a savings account for me. I remember feeling so excited and independent. I loved the idea of having my own money. After that, whenever I received cash as birthday gifts and when I was old enough to work during the summer, I would send a deposit to the bank. By the time I was 18, I had saved enough to put a down payment on my first car.

How was money handled in your household growing up?

Did your parents talk about money?
Did you have a positive or negative experience with money growing up?

Was there the feeling of "enough" in your household or a feeling of "lack"?

What were some of the comments you remember hearing as a child?

We don't have enough money.
Money doesn't grow on trees.
Why does money burn a hole in your pocket?

Did you spend money as soon as you received it?
As you think about the messages you received growing up, how have they impacted you in your adult life?

Beliefs that Steal Your MONEY POWER

Here are some questions to ask yourself:

* What are my beliefs about money that stand in the way of me achieving my vision?
* Am I telling myself that I am not good with money?
* Do I believe that I am worthy of the financial success that I want?

Some limiting beliefs that I hear from women are:

* I am not good with money.
* I can't spend any money because I don't want to become a bag lady.
* No matter what I do, I can't get ahead.
* If it wasn't for my divorce, I would be in a better financial situation.
* If I had a better job, I could handle my finances better.

When you operate from negative beliefs and mindsets, you are acting from a place of lack rather than a path of prosperity. You are allowing your beliefs to steal your MONEY POWER.

It feels like ...

- You are not discerning, both personally and in business, about what you are willing to accept or not.
- You are willing to settle for less than what you deserve.
- you lack the ability to recognize that you are deserving of something better.
- You put the needs of others ahead of your own.

It looks like ...

- You doubt your worth.
  EXAMPLE: You don't feel comfortable charging what you are worth, because you feel you may lose customers.

- You question your ability to succeed and prosper.
  EXAMPLE: You are not sure you can make money doing what you love, so you are willing to stay in a job you've outgrown.

- You blame others for your situation or circumstance.
  EXAMPLE: If you had a better paying job, you would be better with your finances.

- You live in the past.
  EXAMPLE: You are holding on to past hurts, anger, or resentment.

- You procrastinate on financial decisions.
  EXAMPLE: You put off making financial decisions because you just don't want to deal with them.

- You don't ask for help or support.
  EXAMPLE: You are trying to do it all yourself, even though you may feel overwhelmed.

Mindsets that Steal Your MONEY POWER

- You have to work hard or you will never achieve your goals.
  EXAMPLE: Overworking to exhaustion in a need to prove yourself—weekends, nights, etc.

- You have to do things you don't want to do.
  EXAMPLE: Feeling undeserving of having your dreams fulfilled and lacking confidence.

- Agreeing to and accepting treatment … even when it isn't in your own best interest, and even when you know it.
  EXAMPLE: Settling for and staying in a relationship even when it isn't honoring or respectful.

- Fear that you aren't going to get what you want, so why ask for it.
  EXAMPLE: Not asking for a raise. Fear of asking for what you truly want.

- Undervaluing your work.
  EXAMPLE: Not charging what you are worth.

- Letting others talk you out of your vision.
  EXAMPLE: Influenced by outside pressures and opinions of someone who cannot see or understand your vision.

Holding on to Limiting Beliefs

Holding on to limiting beliefs and mindsets that steal your MONEY POWER can…

- Steal your eagerness and enthusiasm to take bold new actions and reach for your full potential in building your business, as well as your personal life.
  EXAMPLE: Your current actions are not focused toward moving you toward your dreams.

- Create a sense of overwhelm or trigger self-doubt.
  EXAMPLE: You aren't trusting your vision (and what you stand for)… not trusting your instincts and your ability to see the steps necessary to achieve your vision, especially outside the "well-intentioned" opinions of others.

- You are not fully expressing your unique gifts.
  EXAMPLE: You are not using your best talents and gifts to do the type of work you love.

Understanding and transforming any limiting beliefs you may have that no longer serve you can help you to overcome them and make healthy financial choices.

Why is it important to develop an empowered relationship with money?

I truly believe that our personal relationship with money directly impacts how successful we can become in our personal and professional lives. When you create a more positive relationship with money, you begin to rise to your MONEY POWER.

You feel ...

- focused on your vision
- confident about your relationship with money
- you have a plan in place to achieve your goals
- your motivation comes from within
- your work serves a higher purpose
- you have a quiet knowing and trust that you are supported by the universe

What money story are you telling? Is it the same old story? For example, "I am not good with money. My family was never good with money. No one in my family has money, so why try? I will never achieve my goals."

The story you tell will be the foundation for your life. It's time to change the story to make it a more positive one. For instance, "I forgive myself for my past financial mistakes. I know I am on the path to financial independence because I have a good plan in place and am taking daily steps to make good financial decisions and improve my finances."

Action Steps:

1. Take my free <u>Money Type Quiz</u> to learn more about your relationship with money.
2. In your journal, write down your first memory of money (good or bad) and how it has impacted your life.
3. Also list the beliefs that you currently have about money that are standing in the way of you achieving your goals.

Chapter 4

STEP TWO:
Nurture a Prosperity Mindset

IN THIS CHAPTER, YOU WILL:

- **Learn** how to create a MONEY POWER Vision and ways to naturally nurture a Prosperity Mindset.
- **Gain** an understanding of how the practice of gratitude amplifies your MONEY POWER.
- **Access** the real meaning of forgiveness to open the flow of your MONEY POWER.

Prosperity is more than how much money you have. It is also about having a successful and thriving life.

Do you focus on the good in your life, or are you focused on scarcity or what is lacking? A prosperity mindset allows you to be content regardless of what's in your bank account.

There are three ways to create a prosperity mindset:

- Create your MONEY POWER VISION
- Practice gratitude
- Embrace forgiveness

What is most important to you? The first step to creating your MONEY POWER VISION is to identify your values. Do your values support your vision?

What is a Value?

A value is a belief, mission, or philosophy that is really meaningful to you.

Some common values include:

- Abundance
- Prosperity
- Financial Freedom
- Security
- Happiness

- No worries
- Helping others
- Independence
- Family/Relationships
- Education
- Spirituality
- Other....

When you identify and reflect on your **top 5 values,** does how you are living your life reflect what's most important to you?

Create Your MONEY POWER VISION

Vision is using your imagination to see what is possible. Your MONEY POWER VISION is your compass. It gives you direction and guides you to where you're headed.

Ask yourself:

- What is my vision for my life (spiritual, career and business, personal, financial security, etc.)?
- What are my unique gifts that I want to bring to the world?
- What impact do I want to make in the world?
- What is my big "why"?
- What does my life look like in 5 years?

- Do I have an unwavering passion for my vision?
- Does my vision reflect my values?

When writing your MONEY POWER VISION, don't limit yourself. Be bold!

Once you create your MONEY POWER VISION, read it at least once a day. It will help you to stay focused on your vision and help to create a positive mindset focused on abundance rather than lack. In addition, creating a vision board to display images that represent whatever you want to be, do, or have in your life helps you to maintain clarity and focus on your life goals.

Does your self-talk support your vision?

You can create positive affirmations to help you to reframe and overcome self-sabotaging and negative thoughts. When you repeat them often and believe in them, you can start to make positive changes. If you constantly think, *I am not good with money*, replace it with *I always make good financial decisions.*

Practice Gratitude

The practice of gratitude amplifies your MONEY POWER. Most of us know that gratitude is the key to growing our inner wealth. But did you know that the inner wealth gives us the power to grow our outer wealth?

I love this quote from Oprah Winfrey: *"Be thankful for what you have; you'll end up having more. If you concentrate on what you don't have, you will never, ever have enough."*

This is so true. It applies to every area of our lives, but I want to focus in particular on how gratitude affects our financial lives. Practicing gratitude at whatever financial stage we are in gives us the patience and motivation to continue moving forward on our journey to financial success.

Here are five ways to practice financial gratitude:

1. Celebrate the present
Staying in gratitude helps you celebrate the present. Celebrating the present helps you stay positive.

2. Be thankful
Be thankful for wherever you are in your financial journey. Being thankful gives you the patience to continue with your plan, which will lead to further financial success.

3. Save
By practicing and staying in the present, you are less likely to spend on impulse or buy things you don't need. The less you spend, the more you have to save toward your financial goals. Set a weekly or monthly savings goal and commit to it.

4. Give

Open a giving account. Set aside a certain amount of your income each month to be given to causes you are passionate about. You can accumulate the money and periodically donate. You will be surprised how fast the funds will grow if you take a systematic approach to saving.

5. Celebrate your financial milestones

It is important to celebrate the large successes, but it is equally important to celebrate small milestones. By celebrating each milestone, it gives you the encouragement to continue with your plan.

It *is* possible to be financially secure and unhappy at the same time. It is equally possible to live modestly and be grateful to be employed and have your needs met. Practicing gratitude daily shifts your focus from lack to a prosperity mindset, and sets you up for future success.

Embrace Forgiveness

Before we go any further, there's a crucial topic I feel must be addressed. And that is the embracing forgiveness...

Embracing forgiveness was one of the most important lessons I learned while going through my divorce. Everything in my life was planned except for the divorce. I felt stuck. I had to deal with a lot of emotions including fear, anger, and resentment. I realized I needed to learn to forgive not only my husband, but also myself in order to move forward. Fortunately, I had a wonderful spiritual teacher at the time who helped me learn the importance of forgiveness.

This is what I learned:

- Not doing the inner work to let go of unhealed wounds, anger, resentment, blame, and hurt can block the flow of prosperity and abundance.
- Through forgiveness, you open yourself up to attracting opportunities and manifesting your goals.
- It is not necessary to forgive the act, just the person.
- Forgiveness clears the negative energy that creates space to help you manifest to your highest good.
- Forgiveness gives you the clarity and energy to take the action steps needed to move forward.

If you are feeling "stuck" personally or financially and trying to move past any hurt, anger, or resentment, here are a couple of questions to ask yourself:

- Who am I holding resentment or anger toward?
- Why am I not letting go?
- Who does my lack of forgiveness hurt the most?
- Am I ready to let go of this?

If you are ready to let go of the energy and move

forward, there is a wonderful and easy practice to start with called **Ho'oponopono**. *Ho'oponopono* is an ancient Hawaiian practice of reconciliation and forgiveness. It consists of only four lines:

1) I'm sorry.
2) Please forgive me.
3) Thank you.
4) I love you.

You don't need to say the phrase out loud, just to yourself. Not only is it important to forgive others, but it is equally important to forgive yourself for whatever mistakes you made financially in the past. Forgiveness gives you the gift of a peaceful heart which, in turn, allows you to have the clarity to move forward.

Action Steps:

1. In your journal, create your five-year MONEY POWER VISION.
2. Create a vision board to support your vision.
3. Start a gratitude journal and list at least five things you are grateful for, either daily or weekly.
4. Write at least three positive affirmations that support your vision, and read them daily.
5. Practice *Ho'oponopono* for forgiveness.

Chapter 5

STEP THREE:
Empower Yourself Through Financial Education and Support

IN THIS CHAPTER, YOU WILL:

- **Learn** how gaining education relates to building your confidence.
- **Uncover** the most empowering step you can take to eliminate fear around money.

- **Access The Five MONEY POWER Must-Knows**
  to educate yourself and immediately gain more
  knowledge to stand stronger in your relationship
  with money.

Trying to do it all yourself could be a big mistake. If you feel overwhelmed or need additional expertise, it is time to consider gaining more knowledge and reaching out for support.

Empowering yourself through financial education helps you make informed decisions. You should make your financial decisions based on sound information, research, or advice—not on emotions such as fear or anxiety.   In addition, education gives you the confidence to handle your finances appropriately.

The most empowering step you can take to eliminate fear around money is to take ownership of your financial future.

The Five MONEY POWER Must-Knows to educate yourself and immediately gain more knowledge to stand stronger in your relationship with money are:

1. **Read**. This includes blogs, magazines, investment newsletters and annual reports. Also go online to review articles.

2. **Review.** Review your portfolio statements and make sure you understand what's in your portfolio and why.

3. **Attend workshops or classes.** There are numerous workshops or financial classes (online or in-person) you can attend to get basic financial literacy. The key is to enroll in a class where they are not trying to sell you a product.

4. **Get support.** Join a community (online or in-person) that is focused on providing education and support to the members.

5. **Consult.** If it feels overwhelming, or you need additional guidance, it may benefit you to seek professional help.

By staying informed and engaged through financial education and support, you can immediately stand stronger in your relationship with money and empower yourself with the knowledge to make good financial decisions.

Action Steps:

1. Read at least one piece of financial information daily.
2. Review your investment statements.
3. Attend a financial workshop.

Chapter 6

STEP FOUR:
Take Inspired Action

IN THIS CHAPTER, YOU WILL:

- **Learn** how self-love can serve as the foundation of your finances.
- **Discover** what it means to take inspired action.
- **Acquire** an understanding of the importance of designing a well-defined **MONEY POWER WEALTH-BUILDING STRATEGY.**

Taking action is the practical side to rising to your MONEY POWER. When you develop a good relationship with money, you ignite true inspiration and can easily and confidently move forward.

We all know the importance of self-care but, as women, we tend to take care of everyone else before we take care of ourselves. In addition, when we think of self-care, we typically think of things like the importance of exercise, taking time for yourself, eating healthy, etc. But what you may not realize is that making sure your finances are in order is also a form of self-care.

Self-love serves as the foundation of your finances. It begins with financial literacy and creating good financial practices.

Action Versus Inspired Action

Taking action is the practical side of rising to your MONEY POWER. You are confident you have a good relationship with money and are ready to put a plan in place to achieve your goals.

When you take inspired action, not only do you have a quiet knowing and trust that you are being supported by the universe, but you also know the steps you are taking are leading you toward your vision.

We need to begin by creating a solid financial foundation. Here are nine steps you can take to build a solid financial foundation:

1. Organize your paperwork
2. Know where you stand financially
3. Create a monthly spending plan
4. Make sure you have adequate insurance coverage
5. Know your credit history
6. Set clear financial goals
7. Protect your assets through smart estate planning
8. Stay informed and engaged
9. Remember your annual review

Step 1: Organize Your Paperwork

One way to simplify your life is to eliminate the clutter by organizing your files and recordkeeping. Getting ready for tax season is the time we typically organize our recordkeeping, but anytime is a good time to eliminate the clutter and get your home recordkeeping in order. When you think in terms of home recordkeeping, there are three main areas you want to focus on:

- Home files and financial records
- Estate planning
- Disaster planning

While organizing your 1099s, end of year statements, and other tax documents, you should also take some time to organize your permanent home files and financial records. The key is to use a filing system that is efficient and easy to maintain. You should update your files at least once a year to determine what should be kept and what should be thrown away. If you are not sure how long documents should be retained, you can go online to find a list.

With identity theft on the rise, it is important to destroy documents appropriately to maintain your privacy.

Estate Planning

You also should think about what estate planning documents you need to maintain and where they will be stored. Your estate planning recordkeeping is not only about your basic estate planning documents such as your will or trust. You can make handling your estate after you're gone less stressful for family members or others by making your wishes known in writing.

Disaster Planning

We don't like to think of dealing with a disaster, but it is also important to think of home recordkeeping in the context of disaster planning. If you've let your recordkeeping get the best of you or you need professional help, you might consider working with a good local professional organizer.

Take the time to simplify your life by eliminating the clutter and organizing your files and recordkeeping. This process will not only simplify your life, but also prepare you for meeting with the professionals you work with (CPA, Financial Planner, Financial Advisor, Attorney).

Action Step: Within one week, you can create an

efficient recordkeeping system and destroy outdated paperwork.

Step 2: Know Where You Stand Financially

Before you can put a plan in place, you need to organize and understand your expenses, savings, debt, etc. You need to know exactly how much is coming in, how much is going out, and how much is left over.

You also need to understand your Net Worth and Cash Flow:

- Net Worth =   Assets   -   Liabilities
- Cash Flow =   Income   -   Expenses

Not only is it important to take the time to create these statements so you have a starting point, but it is also important to include your spouse or significant other in this process. You both should have an understanding of the family finances and be able to set goals as a couple. Either of you should be able to step in and be knowledgeable about everything from the monthly budget to insurance and investments.

Do you have a spouse or significant other?
Earlier in the book, I talked about one of the common ways we give our MONEY POWER away is by letting others manage our finances.

If you are part of a couple, it is important that you talk with your significant other on a regular basis about the family finances.

Here are three tips for starting the conversation with your honey about money:

1. Schedule a "date" to discuss your finances.
Regardless of who is responsible for paying the monthly expenses, it is important to periodically schedule a time to meet with your mate to talk about where you are financially.

- **Monthly**: Review your income and expenses to determine if you are on track to your spending plan. You can easily keep track of this type of information by using a personal finance program.

- **Quarterly**: Review any 401(k)s, IRAs, and brokerage account statements.

  Also check your progress toward your goals. For example, if you are trying to pay down debt or achieve a savings goal, it will help keep you motivated to see that you're making progress.

- **Annually**: Review your strategy to see if you are on target to reach your goals or if adjustments need to be made. If you are working with a financial advisor, schedule a meeting.

2. Make a list of financial items your partner needs to know.

If there was an emergency, would either of you be able to locate your important financial papers? Or even have a handle on the family finances? Make sure you are both protected financially in case something happens to one of you. Create a financial folder with a list of financial items they need to know (i.e., account numbers, contact information, insurance policies and brokerage accounts, etc.).

3. Schedule a meeting with a financial expert.

If you and your honey can't seem to see eye to eye when it comes to finances or the process seems overwhelming, it may benefit you to seek professional help. Being proactive with your significant other when it comes to talking about money not only helps you grow together financially, but it also will help you both gain more confidence in your ability to achieve your long-term goals.

Action step: Within 48 hours, schedule a date with your spouse or significant other to review your household finances.

Step 3: Create a Monthly Spending Plan

Do you know where your money goes? Do you have a positive cash flow? If your answer is no (or "I don't know!") to either of these questions, you need to create a spending plan (budget). We all know how important it is to live within our means, but it is equally important that you are able to identify where your money is being spent.

Creating a spending plan also helps you identify areas where you can potentially reallocate to fund your goals.

Action Step: Within the next two weeks, use a budgeting program to create a monthly budget or spending plan.

Step 4: Make Sure You Have Adequate Insurance Coverage

Protecting your assets in case of an unexpected illness or other event is important. You need to make sure that you have adequate insurance in place. This includes:

- Life
- Health
- Car, home, personal articles
- Liability
- Disability
- Long-term care

Your evaluation should include the cost and terms of your current coverage with a qualified professional. Also consider current deductibles and take into consideration any discount eligibility. In addition, if you are employed, don't forget to review your group policies.

3 Reasons You Need a Long-Term Care Strategy

Having a well-thought-out long-term care strategy is critical to the success of your retirement plan. Not having a long-term care strategy can derail a really good retirement plan. Before you can create a strategy, it is important to understand what long-term care is.

Long-term care is a generic term that covers the services that individuals may need due to age or health-related problems. The individual may need assistance with performing activities of daily living such as bathing, walking, help with taking medication, shopping, cooking, and driving. Long-term care services can be provided in a home, assisted living facility, or nursing home.

Whether you purchase long-term care insurance or choose to self-insure, it is critical that you have a well-thought-out strategy. Here are three reasons why you need a long-term care strategy:

1. Consider these statistics according to longtermcare. org:

- More than half of all seniors will need long-term care.
- The average nursing home stay is 3.7 years and costs run on average between $70,000 to $80,000 per year.

2. Long-term care impacts women both as caregivers and recipients:

- Women as Caregivers: Long-term care affects women who are caregivers. The more time we spend out of the workforce the more it impacts our retirement and other benefits.
- Women Live Longer Than Men: On average, women outlive men by about 5 years. A healthy 65-year-old woman can expect to live another 21 years to age 86. One of every four 65-year-olds today will live to age 90 (wiserwomen.org).

3. To ensure you have future care when you are no longer able to take care of yourself, you must be able to answer three questions:

- What type of care do you want?
- Do you want to stay in your home as long as possible?
- How will you pay for your care?

There are basically three options for funding your long-term care services:

- Out of your own pocket—this option can be very expensive

- Medicaid covers long-term care for low-income individuals
- Long-term care insurance policy

Typically, you should start thinking about creating your strategy in your mid-forties to early fifties. Whether you purchase long-term care insurance or choose to self-insure, it is critical that you have a well-thought-out strategy.

Action Step: Within a week, gather and organize your policies and statements.

Step 5: Know Your Credit History

Maintaining a good credit history is one of the most important steps you can take. One of the main ways to accomplish this is to take steps to reduce credit card and other high-interest debt.

Questions you need to answer:

- **Do you have credit in your own name?** You should have at least one credit card solely in your name.

- **Are you using credit wisely?** Do you pay off your balances monthly, or carry them from month to month? It is a good practice to pay off your credit card balances each month, if possible. If you can't pay off your balance, this is a good time to put a strategy in place to pay down your debt. Just adding an additional $100 to your minimum payment can make a big difference in decreasing the amount of interest and number of years to pay off. Use an online debt calculator to help you estimate how long it will take to pay off your credit card debt.

- **Is your credit report accurate?** You don't want to wait until you apply for credit to find out your credit report is inaccurate. A good practice is to request a copy of your credit report at least annually. You are entitled to one free credit report per year. Go to http://www.annualcreditreport.com.

Action Step: Within 24 hours, order a copy of your credit report and review for accuracy.

Step 6: Set Clear Financial Goals

Having discussed the first three foundational steps, it is time to set your financial goals. Regardless of what stage of life we are in, we all need to have financial goals. If you are part of a couple, it is important that you and your significant other are on the same page regarding your financial goals.

What is most important to you? Before you get started,

take a minute to visualize what your life looks like after you have achieved your financial goal.

Whether your goal is to take a once-in-a-lifetime vacation, retire, or create an emergency fund, you need to estimate how much money you need to fund the goal. Because you likely will have multiple goals, it is also important to prioritize them.

Re-read your MONEY POWER VISION and translate it into specific goals you would like to accomplish not only financially, but for each area of your life (spiritual, health, relationships, professional, and financial).

Vision without goals and a solid action plan is just a dream.

Some of the common goals that I hear people say include, "I want to…"

- Pay down debt
- Purchase a first or second home
- Start a business
- Achieve financial independence
- Increase income in retirement
- Not outlive my money
- Leave a legacy to my children
- Increase my financial security
- Take a vacation

- Reduce the amount of time spent worrying about finances

You want to avoid setting vague goals. Goals should be SMART (specific, measurable, achievable, realistic, and time-bound). For example, *My goal is to build an emergency fund,* versus *My goal is to increase my emergency fund to $12,000 within 12 months.*

Here are three factors that determine your financial goals:

1. Your Priorities (values)

Examples:

- *Independence*
- *Quality of life*
- *Early retirement*
- *Give to a charity*

2. Your Responsibilities (items part of your monthly cash flow)

Examples:

- *Children's education*
- *Support for elderly parents*
- *Car loans*

3. Your Dreams (your MONEY POWER VISION and aspirations)

Examples:

- *Second home*

- *Travel*
- *Leave a legacy*

As you go through the process of setting and prioritizing your goals, take all three factors into consideration. It may be helpful to use a goals worksheet.

Setting Goals Is a Process

The most important step toward creating your financial foundation is to set clear financial goals. Your goals help you move toward your MONEY POWER VISION and measure your progress. But goals are not static and may change over time, so it is important to revisit them on a periodic basis.

Action Step: Within the next week, sit down in a quiet place and take some time to set at least three SMART financial goals (short, intermediate and long-term).

Step 7: Protect Your Assets Through Smart Estate Planning

Just like planning for retirement, estate planning is a woman's issue because, in general, we live longer and we typically marry spouses who are older.

If you don't have a strategy for your estate, the government has one for you. Here are some key actions you should take:

- Meet with your attorney regularly
- Prepare estate planning documents
- Review and update beneficiary designations
- Make sure investments are titled appropriately
- Don't forget about your charitable giving

Action Step: In the next two weeks, schedule a meeting with an estate planning professional to create or update your estate plan.

Step 8: Stay Informed and Engaged

By staying informed and engaged, you can empower yourself with the knowledge to make good financial decisions.

- **Read.** This includes magazines, investment newsletters and annual reports. Also go online to review articles.

- **Review.** Review your portfolio statements and make sure you understand what's in your portfolio and why.

- **Consult.** Work with a CFP® professional who is

dedicated to using the financial planning process to serve your financial needs.

Step 9: Remember Your Annual Review

Just like your annual trip to the doctor can provide vital health information and help identify issues before they become serious, the same can be said for your annual financial reviews.

In addition, goals and priorities sometimes change, so it is important that you review your financial plan on an annual basis to make sure you are on track to meet your long-term financial goals.

Action Step: Annually review your plan to see if you are still on track.

Designing a Well-Defined MONEY POWER WEALTH- BUILDING STRATEGY

Once you've built your foundation, you should focus on creating a well-defined MONEY POWER WEALTH- BUILDING STRATEGY. But what's involved? Are you building wealth, or just saving money? It's important to understand the difference. Saving is important for building your emergency fund or for short-term goals. But what's involved in building wealth? Building wealth is about making your money work for you.

It consists of five steps:

1. Make Money
2. Spend Less
3. Reduce Debt
4. Save More
5. Create Your Investment Plan

Make Money

By using your best talents and gifts to do the work you love, you become open to attracting all the ideas, resources, people, opportunities, and situations to help you achieve your vision. In addition, by charging what you are worth, you attract those who need and value the gifts you are bringing to the world.

Financial prosperity enables you to share your abundance with those you love, as well as support causes you are passionate about.

Spend Less

Stay up to date on where you are financially. Earlier, I discussed the importance of creating your spending plan to achieve your financial goals. It is important to review your spending plan periodically to identify areas where you can reduce your spending to redirect funds toward your goals.

Reduce Your Debt

Reducing your debt allows you to redirect more funds toward savings and building wealth.

Save More

Once you have committed to a savings plan as part of building your foundation, commit to maximizing your savings. As your income increases, so should your savings.

Create an Investment Plan

The first step to creating your investment plan is to understand the basics of investing, how to make investment decisions, and the process of creating an investment plan. In addition, it is also important to build a longevity plan into protecting your wealth.

Five steps you can take to create an investment plan are:

1. Take an active role in your investments
2. Create a solid retirement plan
3. Invest for growth
4. Take a systematic approach to investing
5. Choosing to work with a financial professional

Take an Active Role in Your Investments

As you develop your investment plan, you will need to explore questions such as:

- What is your current life stage and lifestyle?
- What are your primary investment goals?
- What is your investment time horizon?
- Given your goals and time frame, which types and levels of investment risk are appropriate for you?

If you are still working:

- Take an active interest in your investments
- Invest early and often
- Capitalize on tax-advantaged retirement planning vehicles
- Contribute as much as you can to your retirement plans
- Invest for growth
- Review your social security benefit statement annually

If you are retired:

- Be smart with your spending
- Set aside cash reserves (1-2 years)
- Consider the tax implications of withdrawals

- Protect your portfolio against the rising costs of healthcare
- Stay diversified
- Stay flexible about withdrawals

Remember, inflation influences what you can spend and how your money is invested, especially in retirement.

One of the best ways to start building wealth is to create a retirement plan.

One of the most common goals people have is to live a successful retirement. But how do you know if you are on track? Here are five ways to maximize your retirement savings:

1. **Invest early and often:** The younger you are when you start contributing to your retirement plans, the less you need to save. The key is to just start with what you can afford and contribute on a regular basis by setting up an automatic transfer from your account or paycheck to fund your IRA or 401(k).

2. **Contribute to the appropriate type of retirement account:**

If you're working: Take advantage of the 401(k) or other employer-sponsored retirement plans such as a 403(b) or 457 plan.

If you're married, but don't work outside the home: Make contributions to a spousal IRA.

If you're self-employed: Are you saving for retirement? If so, do you have the right type of plan? Don't overlook the retirement plan options available to you (i.e., SEP IRA, Owner 401(k), etc.). This is one of the best strategies for building wealth outside your business.

3. **Maximize your contributions:** If you cannot contribute the maximum, just start with what you can afford and build from there. A good strategy is to increase your contribution each time you receive a raise until you reach the maximum contribution. If you receive bonuses, use part of the bonus to contribute to an IRA.

4. **Consolidate your retirement accounts:** Consider talking with your advisor about consolidating multiple IRAs and rolling over 401(k)s from previous employers. If you are no longer with the company, your money shouldn't be there either. By consolidating into an IRA, you'll give yourself more flexibility in terms of investment options and have a better picture of your portfolio.

5. **Determine whether you are on track to meet your goals:** It is important to know how much money you need to fund your retirement and track your progress at least annually. You can use an online ballpark estimate tool to determine whether you are currently on track.

Plan for a longer rather than shorter retirement

Retirement can be one of the most rewarding stages

of your life. Unfortunately, if you don't plan for a long retirement, you can run the risk of outliving your money. Did you know…

- If you are 65, your life expectancy is 85.6, and
- One of every four 65-year-olds today will live to age 90.4?

Retirement planning is not just about the numbers. It starts with your goals. What does retirement look like for you?

You are in control…

You are in control of your financial future. Careful planning and a long-term strategy can go a long way toward achieving your long-term retirement goals and living the retirement lifestyle you desire.

Invest for Growth

The risk of being overly conservative with your investments is that you potentially could outlive your money. You should invest based on your risk tolerance and time horizon, but not be overly conservative. Consider investing at least part of your portfolio for growth.

Take a Systematic Approach to Investing

Taking a systematic approach to investing is key to

becoming a better investor; it is not about how much you invest. It is more about creating a solid investment plan. Here are seven steps to help you create a better portfolio and become a better investor:

1. Know your "why."

The first step to investing is to know "why." You should have established a long-term investment goal such as planning for retirement. If you anticipate needing the funds sooner than 5 to 7 years, then the funds should not be invested.

2. Understand how much risk you are willing to take.

A few years ago, I met with a new client to review her portfolio. When I asked her how she felt about the risk she was taking in her portfolio, she replied, "I can't sleep at night because of worrying about my portfolio." Her portfolio was more aggressive than she felt comfortable with. So, we made changes to the portfolio to put it more in line with her risk tolerance and time horizon.

You need to understand and be comfortable with the amount of risk you are willing to take in your portfolio. In addition, it needs to make sense based on your goals and time horizon.

3. Be well-diversified.

Having investments in different asset classes in your portfolio reduces the overall risk in your portfolio.

4. Choose quality investments.

In addition to having a well-diversified portfolio, it is important to choose quality investments. Investments paying an abnormally high yield or dividend may be attractive, but remember the saying, "If it sounds too good to be true, it probably is."

5. Keep a long-term perspective.

When creating your investment strategy, it is important to have a long-term perspective based on your goals and risk tolerance. You will be more likely to stick to a long-term strategy and not tempted to sell investments at the wrong time.

6. Focus on what you can control.

Focusing on what you can control is key when it comes to your investments. There are a lot of things you cannot control, including the market (whether it is up or down) and the economy, but what you can control are the first five strategies indicated above. There will always be some news headlines affecting the market in the short-term, but by focusing on what you can control and your long-term strategy, you won't need to worry about the day-to-day noise.

7. Partner with a financial professional.

If you need additional support or advice, consider partnering with a financial professional.

What to Consider When Working with a Financial Professional

If you are considering working with a financial planner, there are three areas to consider:

1. The benefits of working with a financial planner
2. Choosing a financial planner
3. What to bring to the meeting

The benefits of working with a financial planner

A financial planning professional can help you translate your information into some realistic goals so they can develop strategies that make sense for you. The key benefits of working with a financial planner are they:

- Help you identify and set realistic goals and objectives.
- Evaluate your current financial situation by examining your assets, liabilities, income, insurance, taxes, investments and estate plan.
- Develop a comprehensive plan to meet your financial goals.
- Implement your plan.
- Monitor the plan to help yourself stay on track to meet your long-term financial goals.

Choosing a financial planner

It is important to work with an advisor you trust and who truly understands you, your goals, and your situation. You not only want to work with someone who is competent and ethical, but who also puts your needs first. It is also important to understand what type of financial advice the professional will be providing to you. Are they willing to take a comprehensive approach to your financial situation? Working with a Certified Financial Planner™ professional is beneficial. A CFP® professional is dedicated to using the financial planning process to serve your financial needs. Not everyone needs a comprehensive financial plan, but everyone can benefit from the process.

In your initial meeting with a financial planner, there are key questions you should ask to determine if they are a good fit for you. You need to understand the planner's:

- Designations & Licenses
- Education
- Experience
- Fees & Compensation
- Services & Work Philosophy

What to bring to the meeting

It's important to be prepared when you meet with a financial planner. Once you and the financial planner have decided it's appropriate to work together, they will give you a customized list of financial documents needed to perform their analysis.

A common misconception some individuals have is that you need to be wealthy to work with a financial planner. That is not true. Everyone deserves to have a financial plan in place to help them live a comfortable life. It is a matter of finding the right professional for your situation.

If you choose to work with an investment advisor

There are four key benefits of having professional advice in establishing an investment plan once your financial plan is in place.

The professional can:

- Build a portfolio tailored to your needs and goals
- Help you understand the risks
- Adjust your portfolio and investments when necessary
- Help you keep a long-term perspective

It is important to work with an advisor you trust and that truly understands you, your goals, and your situation. Get advice based on what's best for you, partner with your investment advisor, and understand what you are paying for.

Whether you decide to manage your portfolio yourself or work with a financial professional, it is important for you to stay engaged around your investments. Staying informed and engaged goes a long way toward helping you become a better investor, and it empowers you with the knowledge to make good financial decisions.

When Should I Update My Plan?

Not only is it important to create a solid financial plan to get you to your goals, but it is also important to update your plan periodically. Your financial plan should be reviewed and updated on an annual basis and/or as your goals change. You may have experienced recent changes since completing your plan. We all have a lot of changes that occur in our lives, but there are certain life changes that affect us financially as well. To be successful in achieving your financial goals, you need to update your financial plan when you have a major life change.

Here are six major life stages when you need to update your financial strategy:

1. Marriage
Now that you are sharing your lives and financial responsibilities, you need to update your financial plan. For various reasons, we sometimes have the tendency to not want to talk with our significant other about financial matters. It is important that you both understand the family finances and are able to set goals as a couple. Either of you should be able to step in and

be knowledgeable about everything from the monthly budget to insurance and investments.

2. Divorce
Divorce can be a difficult time not only emotionally, but also when it comes to finances. Whether you are trying to maintain your financial situation or getting back on your feet, there are some key areas of your financial plan that need updating:

- Know where you stand financially
- Create a budget
- Review credit reports
- Your emergency fund
- Your estate plan

3. Children
Adding children to your family is exciting. Whether you're expecting, thinking about adoption, or building a blended family, you need to plan for the added expenses. According to the U.S. Department of Agriculture's 2017 report, the typical middle-income family will spend on average $233,610 to raise a child born in 2015 through age 17.

You may now need to revise your budget to accommodate expenses such as childcare or to allow one parent to stay home. You also need to review your insurance policies and estate plan to make sure your family is protected. You may also want to reallocate resources to start funding for college.

4. Career or Job Change

Whether you have experienced the loss of a job or are considering accepting a new job offer, it is a good time to talk with your financial planner about your key financial concerns.

Losing a job can be stressful, but it doesn't have to be financially devastating. Whether you were unemployed due to termination, merger, or layoff, the key financial concerns may include loss of income, medical and other benefits.

Or, you may be currently employed, but considering a career or job change. You want to consider how this new job will affect your current retirement plan or whether or not the benefits package is sufficient to meet your family's needs.

5. Retirement

Retirement can be one of the most rewarding stages of your life. Unfortunately, if you don't plan properly, you can run the risk of not living the retirement you envisioned. This is a good time to meet with a financial planner to update the answers to key questions such as: *How much have I saved?* and *How long will my money last?*

6. Death of a Spouse

Dealing with the death of a spouse can be overwhelming both emotionally and financially. You will need to compile a list of tasks and issues that will need to be addressed. Your financial planner, along with your estate planning attorney, can help you through this process.

A financial plan is not a static document...

It should be reviewed and updated on an annual basis and/or as your goals change. It is also important that you revisit and update your plan when you have major life changes. If you have had a major life change recently, now is a good time to schedule a meeting with your CERTIFIED FINANCIAL PLANNER™ professional.

Self-love related to your finances begins with financial literacy and creating good financial practices. Putting solid financial practices in place can go a long way toward helping you achieve the life you envision.

Action Steps:

1. Create a financial calendar.
2. Review your Social Security Benefit Statement.
3. Review your 401k statements and other retirement assets.
4. Update your financial plan, if needed.

Chapter 7

STEP FIVE:
Create Your Money Power Manifesto

IN THIS CHAPTER, YOU WILL:

- **Discover** why it is vital to have a personal **MONEY POWER MANIFESTO.**
- **Learn** the steps to define your personal **MONEY POWER MANIFESTO.**
- **Find** out how to put your personal **MONEY POWER MANIFESTO** into action.

*By creating a **MONEY POWER MANIFESTO**...
by giving language to your vision, intentions, and
motivations... you will naturally focus on what you want
to create for your future.*

What is a manifesto? It's a verbal declaration of intentions
and motivations. And in this case, it is a manifesto
guiding you to own your MONEY POWER, simply,
easily—and beginning today.

A MONEY POWER MANIFESTO is a collection of
intentional statements that declare your vision around
how you are rising to your MONEY POWER.

It is vital to have a personal MONEY POWER
MANIFESTO because it provides you with a daily
practice to help you stay motivated and inspired. It
helps you to keep the momentum going in shifting
your beliefs about money, inspiring clarity, confidence,
and focus on where you want to be in your relationship
with money.

The steps to define your personal MONEY POWER
MANIFESTO include:

1. Write your intention statement around money.
2. Identify and write the affirmations or declarations
   that will lead you to your intention.

Here is a MONEY POWER MANIFESTO to help inspire you to write your own:

I AM RISING IN MY MONEY POWER.
Today I will create a more empowered
relationship with money.
I know that my personal relationship with
money directly impacts how successful I am.
I will eliminate any limiting beliefs about money
that are holding me back personally
and professionally.
Developing a good relationship with money
is fueling my eagerness, enthusiasm, and
confidence to take bold new actions.
I am creating the life I deserve and
the financial success I desire.

Post your MONEY POWER MANIFESTO in a prominent location and make reading it a daily practice. Putting your personal MONEY POWER MANIFESTO into action helps you to naturally focus on what you want to create for your future.

Now, live your MONEY POWER MANIFESTO. And work it!

Action Steps:

1. In your journal or on a separate sheet of paper, create your own MONEY POWER MANIFESTO.
2. Post it on your wall or another place where you can easily see it.
3. Read it daily.

Chapter 8

Moving Forward on Your Money Power Journey

It is important, now more than ever, that you bring your gifts into the world in ways for them to have the greatest impact.

Without even realizing it, I think this quote has been a mantra for my life:

"Not everyone can be famous but everybody can be great, because anybody can serve. You don't have to have a college degree to serve. You don't have to make your subject and verb agree to serve. You only need a heart full of grace. A soul generated by love."

~ Martin Luther King Jr.

Having grown up as an army brat, you could say I was destined for a life of service. My father's time in the U.S. Army opened up a wealth of opportunities, travel, diverse cultures, and new people. Most importantly, it contributed to my lifelong commitment to helping others, including becoming a Girl Scout and later pursuing my own service to our country in the Marine Corps.

My vision to serve has been unwavering, but how it has manifested has evolved over the years. First and foremost through the work I do, but also through my philanthropic work in donating my time, talents, and gifts to serve the causes that I support through volunteer activities, serving on boards and raising money for various non-profit organizations.

When you operate from inside your MONEY POWER, you use your grand, beautiful vision as your compass. You will not only inspire others, but also discover unexpected connections, support, ideas, and awareness to help you achieve your goals. In every moment you are choosing to recognize and honor your sense of clarity and range of focus, you are bringing your gifts into the world in ways for them to have the greatest impact.

Are you ready to begin operating from inside your MONEY POWER?

As I mentioned at the beginning of this book, what I deeply desire is to inspire a cultural shift in the consciousness of women to transform their relationship with money, so they can rise in their power by overcoming limiting beliefs, challenges, and self-sabotage related to their work, money, and purpose.

This is my intention for you. This is my intention for all women.

Congratulations on rising to your MONEY POWER!

About the Author

Known as the "Money Mentor for Women," Pamela Plick specializes in helping women find their Money Power, providing education, strategies, and tools to grow financial confidence, security, and freedom.

Pamela Plick is a CERTIFIED FINANCIAL PLANNER (CFP)™ practitioner, Certified Money Coach (CMC)®, and fee-only Registered Investment Advisor. Pamela also holds the specialized professional designation of Certified Divorce Financial Analyst™ and Accredited Wealth Management Advisor™ based in Palm Desert, California. Her firm offers advisory services in the State of California and other jurisdictions where exempted, and specializes in financial education, proactive planning, and wealth management services for women.

Pamela brings over 25 years of experience in the financial services industry to her firm; starting her career at a commercial bank, spending 10 of her years there in the Global Wealth and Investment Management Division, and then as a Financial Advisor with a brokerage firm managing investments. She achieved her dream of starting her own practice in 2011, Pamela Plick Wealth Management LLC.

Her firm's approach and focus is simple, partnering

with savvy and financially independent women to help them achieve their financial goals through education, proactive planning, and investment management. As someone who personally understands the difficulties of taking control of finances after a major life change, Pamela has an unwavering passion for and dedication to empowering and educating women who are beginning the next chapter of their lives about their finances, so they can take charge of their money and live the life they've earned.

Pamela is able to offer her educational services to a greater audience through money coaching and instruction at several universities, institutes, and business centers, as well as hosting Women and Money Workshops, professional speaking engagements, and published articles. Pamela is actively involved in several professional organizations, including the Financial Planning Association. She is a past president of the FPA of the Inland Empire Chapter. Pamela has a commitment to serving her community. Her charitable activities have included raising money for non-profits and serving on several advisory councils related to women's empowerment, health, and education.

Pamela holds a Bachelor of Science degree in Business Administration, with a major in Finance and a minor in Accounting from California State University, Los Angeles. Pamela previously served as adjunct faculty for several universities: The University of Redlands, California State University, San Bernardino, and The Osher Lifelong Learning Institute at California State University, San Bernardino, Palm Desert Campus.

Pamela's work has been featured in *The Huffington Post*, *Golden Girl Finance*, *Investopedia*, *Forbes,* and *USA Today.* She has been interviewed on several national radio outlets, and has been a featured expert on *NerdWallet*, *Golden Girl Finance,* and *DailyWorth.*

Other Books by Pamela Plick

Pamela has contributed to the following books:

Dear Amazing Daughter: Awakening a NEW Conversation About Becoming the Amazing Women We Are Meant To Be, Marsh Engle, 2018

Rise. Amazing Woman. Rise.: The Eight Essential Powers of the Feminine Heart, Marsh Engle, 2019

Lead. Amazing Woman. Lead.: The Eight Essential Powers for Mastering Your Mission, Marsh Engle, 2020

Connect with the Author

Website: http:/www.PamelaPlick.com

Email: pamela@pamelaplick.com

Social Media:

Twitter: https://twitter.com/PamelaPlick

Facebook: https://www.facebook.com/PamelaPlickCFP

LinkedIn: https://linkedin.com/in/PamelaPlick

Pamela Plick on YouTube:
https://www.youtube.com/channel/
UCDwjwyzlgEl514BqiHsY3Mw

References

American Psychological Association. "Divorce." *APA. org.* 2019.

LongTermCare.gov. https://longtermcare.acl.gov

Money Coaching Institute. "The Money Archetype Quiz."

National Center for Health Statistics. "Mortality in the United States." *CDC.gov.* 2016.

Social Security. "Social Security for Women." *SSA.gov.* 2019.

WISER, Women's Institute For A Secure Retirement. "Home." *Wiserwoman.org.* 2019.

Resources

Take my free Money Type quiz: http://moneyquiz.pamelaplick.com/

Watch my Rise to Your Money Power Conversation Series on my YouTube Channel:
https://www.youtube.com/watch?v=NX6dol-665Wk&list=PLdXsXafVRuWIn4idHpxVbN_DKjLZcrK_K

SocialSecurity.gov: https://www.ssa.gov/people/women/

WISER, Women's Institute For A Secure Retirement: http://www.wiserwomen.org/index.php?id=1&page=Home

www.ingramcontent.com/pod-product-compliance
Lightning Source LLC
Chambersburg PA
CBHW022108210326
41521CB00029B/320